SPOTLIGHT ON EXPLORERS AND COLONIZATION™

HERNANDO DE SOTO

First European to Cross the Mississippi

ROBERT Z. COHEN

ROSEN
PUBLISHING®

New York

Published in 2017 by The Rosen Publishing Group, Inc.
29 East 21st Street, New York, NY 10010

First Edition

Library of Congress Cataloging-in-Publication Data

Names: Cohen, Robert Z., author.
Title: Hernando de Soto: First European to Cross the Mississippi / Robert Z. Cohen.
Description: First edition. | New York : Rosen Publishing, [2017] | Series:
  Spotlight on explorers and colonization | Includes bibliographical
  references and index.
Identifiers: LCCN 2016018199| ISBN 9781508172123 (library bound) | ISBN
  9781508172109 (pbk.) | ISBN 9781508172116 (6-pack)
Subjects: LCSH: Soto, Hernando de, approximately 1500–1542—Juvenile
  literature. | Explorers—America—Biography—Juvenile literature. |
  Explorers—Spain—Biography—Juvenile literature. |
  Peru—History—Conquest, 1522–1548—Juvenile literature. | Indians of
  North America—First contact with Europeans—Southern States—Juvenile
  literature. | Southern States—Discovery and
  exploration—Spanish—Juvenile literature. | America—Discovery and
  exploration—Spanish—Juvenile literature.
Classification: LCC E125.S7 C65 2016 | DDC 970.01/6092 [B] —dc23
LC record available at https://lccn.loc.gov/2016018199

Manufactured in China

CONTENTS

A YOUNG HIDALGO'S DREAM

When Christopher Columbus landed on the tiny Caribbean island of San Salvador in October 1492, Spain was a kingdom hungry for an empire. The Spanish king and queen engaged soldiers to discover and conquer new lands for Spain and the Catholic Church. They were known as the conquistadors.

Hernando de Soto was, perhaps, the boldest of all conquistadors. He was born around 1500 in the small town of Jerez de Caballeros, near Badajoz in the poor Spanish province of Extremadura. This was the birthplace of many conquistadors. De Soto's family was poor, but he was born into

Hernando de Soto rose from poverty to become one of Spain's richest nobles and a figure who would change the course of American history.

the hidalgo class—the lowest class of nobles—who were expected to find wealth and fame by the sword rather than by work.

Around 1514, a teenage de Soto joined the expedition of Pedro Arias de Avila—also known as Pedrarias—to colonize the Darién jungle of Panama. It was Spain's first large colonial expedition—1,500 people on nineteen caravel ships.

SERVING THE WRATH OF GOD

Pedrarias—who was nicknamed "the Anger of God"—was a cruel, jealous leader, already old when he sailed for Panama. Under his command, the young de Soto grew to be a tough fighter and skilled horseman.

Personal rivalries were fierce between greedy Spanish leaders. In 1511, the explorer Vasco Núñez de Balboa announced that he had found gold in Panama, triggering an outbreak of "gold fever" in Spain. De Soto showed skill and bravery and rose to the rank of captain at the age of nineteen.

In 1519, de Soto joined the expedition of Gaspar de Espinosa to conquer the

Gaspar de Espinosa taught de Soto to survive and win by any means possible, even if it meant using dishonorable military tactics.

gold-rich land of the Coiba people in northern Panama. Espinosa taught de Soto to combine friendship with treachery, first befriending native chiefs and then kidnapping them, and to use trained cavalry horses and war dogs to terrorize Native Americans. De Soto would use these tactics against Native Americans throughout his future military career.

GOLD FEVER

Exciting news arrived in 1520: Hernán Cortés had found Aztec gold in Mexico. Governor Pedrarias wanted to seek gold in Nicaragua. Other conquistador captains plotted to launch their own gold-seeking raids there, too. De Soto refused to join them and informed Pedrarias of the betrayal. De Soto helped crush the "revolt of the captains" and was rewarded by the governor with a large estate in the new town of León, Nicaragua.

In León, de Soto raided villages for Native American slaves. The native people died in large numbers from diseases introduced by the invaders because Native Americans lacked immunity against common diseases

Once a good friend of de Soto, Francisco Pizarro would soon betray his ally and block de Soto's rise to power.

from Europe, such as the cold and flu viruses.

In 1527, Francisco Pizarro, a close friend of de Soto's, sent ships to search the Pacific coast for the legendary gold of Birú. Near Ecuador, they captured a large Inca sailing raft made of reeds with woven sails. On board, the Spanish found more gold than they had ever seen.

THE GOLDEN EMPIRE

Once ashore, the Spanish found the Inca city of Tumbes, with stone buildings and temples filled with gold. Pizarro quickly sailed to Spain with the news. The king granted Pizarro the right to conquer Peru, but Pedrarias jealously forbade any of his men from joining Pizarro.

Pedrarias soon died of old age, and de Soto joined Pizarro in Tumbes in 1531 with three ships filled with veterans from his Nicaragua campaigns. De Soto's arrival swelled Pizarro's Spanish forces in Peru to about two hundred foot soldiers and one hundred horsemen. Pizarro had promised de Soto he would lead the expedition, but then named his brother Hernando Pizarro as

Imported Old World diseases like smallpox and malaria caused widespread death among Native Americans. Some had reached the Inca even before the Spaniards did!

general. De Soto never again allowed himself to trust in Pizarro's leadership.

While the Pizarro brothers remained behind, de Soto advanced to the rich city of Tumbes to find it empty—a victim of the Europeans' epidemic diseases and a civil war that was raging across the Inca Empire.

THE INCA CIVIL WAR

The Inca King Huayna Capac had warned his two sons about the coming of the Spanish before he died of smallpox in Quito in 1527. His sons—Huascar and Atahualpa—fought over the Inca throne. Atahualpa, who became king, was marching toward Cuzco when his spies informed him of the conquistador advance. With an army eighty thousand strong, he saw no reason to fear three hundred Spaniards.

In October 1532, Pizarro sent de Soto ahead with a small patrol to follow the paved Inca road to the town of Caja, where an ambassador from Atahualpa awaited them with a gift of skinned ducks, which turned

The conquistadors encountered the Inca Empire at its weakest time—following a civil war between the sons of its greatest king.

out to be a symbol of the Inca king's contempt.

The Spanish marched with a mere one hundred soldiers and sixty-eight horsemen. On November 15, 1533, Pizarro and de Soto reached Cajamarca. The bravest horseman—de Soto—rode out to meet the king. De Soto's bravery impressed the king, and he agreed to visit Pizarro the next day.

TREACHERY IN CAJAMARCA

Vastly outnumbered, the Spanish laid a trap, hiding in buildings surrounding the plaza of Cajamarca. Atahualpa came on a peace mission, so his troops carried no weapons. A Spanish priest walked into the plaza declaring that the king of Spain now claimed possession of this new kingdom. Suddenly, the Spanish burst from their hiding places into the square, slashing with their metal swords and firing arquebuses into the plaza. Eight thousand unarmed Inca warriors were massacred. Atahualpa was captured and imprisoned by Pizarro in the Temple of the Sun. Without their Sun King to lead them, the Inca armies were lost.

The capture of Atahualpa sent the Inca world into chaos. Without a strong leader the empire was helpless.

Seeing the Spanish loot Cajamarca's temples for gold, Atahualpa came up with a plan. He called Pizarro into his room and drew a chalk line on the wall as high as he could reach. Atahualpa promised Pizarro that he would fill the room to that mark with gold and silver if he were allowed to live and return in peace to Quito. Pizarro agreed and assigned Hernando de Soto to serve as Atahualpa's personal guard.

De Soto had gained the trust of Atahualpa, and the Inca king's murder was a sign that de Soto could no longer trust Pizarro.

For eight months, pack trains of llamas carried gold treasure to Cajamarca. As the temple filled with riches, Atahualpa realized he would not be freed. Pizarro believed Atahualpa was plotting a surprise attack, and in July 1533, after sending de Soto away on a mission, Pizarro had the Inca king killed. De Soto was angry at the betrayal of the Inca king and now resented Pizarro's command.

Pizarro named Atahualpa's nephew Manco the new Sun King of the Inca and sent de Soto to advance toward the Inca capitol of Cuzco. The Inca army had no defense against the cavalry charges by de Soto's horsemen. Without a king to lead them, the Inca army slowly dispersed and faded away.

BETRAYAL IN CUZCO

On November 15, 1533, the Spanish entered Cuzco. Many of the Cuzco Inca people were Atahualpa's enemies, and they welcomed the Spanish as liberators. Meanwhile, the Spanish helped themselves to more gold than they had ever seen before.

Hernando de Soto was appointed lieutenant governor of Cuzco in August 1534. He soon fell in love with Huascar's daughter, Princess Tocto Chimpu, who was said to be the most beautiful woman in Peru. Together the lovers had a daughter, Leonor, whose descendants in Cuzco carried the name de Soto for generations.

In 1535, Diego de Almagro, who was both a partner and rival of Pizarro's, arrived from Nicaragua to prepare for an invasion of Chile.

De Soto, as imagined by a twentieth-century painter. Like many conquistadors, his descendants still live in Peru.

Almagro and Pizarro argued over the control of Cuzco. Seeing that he had no future in Peru, de Soto took many of his Nicaraguan veterans with him when he packed up his gold and left for Spain.

AT THE COURT OF KING CHARLES

In the spring of 1536, de Soto arrived in Spain, hailed as a hero, the boldest of all conquistadors. Now thirty-six years old, Hernando de Soto married Isabel Bobadilla—the daughter of Pedrarias—an influential friend of Queen Isabella.

In April 1537, King Charles named de Soto governor of Cuba and offered him the right of conquest to a new land that had proved difficult to conquer: La Florida. Juan Ponce de León had failed to establish a colony there in 1513. Then in 1527, Pánfilo de Narváez, the conqueror of Cuba and Jamaica, landed a full invasion force of six hundred men near Tampa Bay, in Florida.

Pánfilo de Narváez's 1527 expedition to Florida was a disaster. Four survivors washed up in Mexico six years later with mysterious tales of "cities of gold."

After marching north to the land of the Apalachee tribe, Narváez and his men were never seen again.

Nine years later, Spanish slave raiders in northwest Mexico attacked a Native American camp and captured a tattooed man who spoke Spanish. It was Álvar Núñez Cabeza de Vaca, one of four survivors of the Narváez expedition.

Cabeza de Vaca, along with an African man named Esteban, had been captured and enslaved by Native Americans and traded among tribes as curiosities. Together they survived and trekked to Mexico. De Soto met Cabeza de Vaca in Spain and asked him to join his mission to Florida. Cabeza de Vaca wisely refused.

When de Soto arrived in Cuba in June 1538, he began recruiting every young man he could find who had not already left for Peru or Mexico. He enlisted blacksmiths, carpenters, tailors, and shipbuilders. All were needed for such an expedition.

In late 1538, de Soto sent Juan de Añasco with two small ships to scout the Florida coast for a suitably deep harbor. Two months later, Añasco returned with four captured Timucua Native Americans. They could not speak

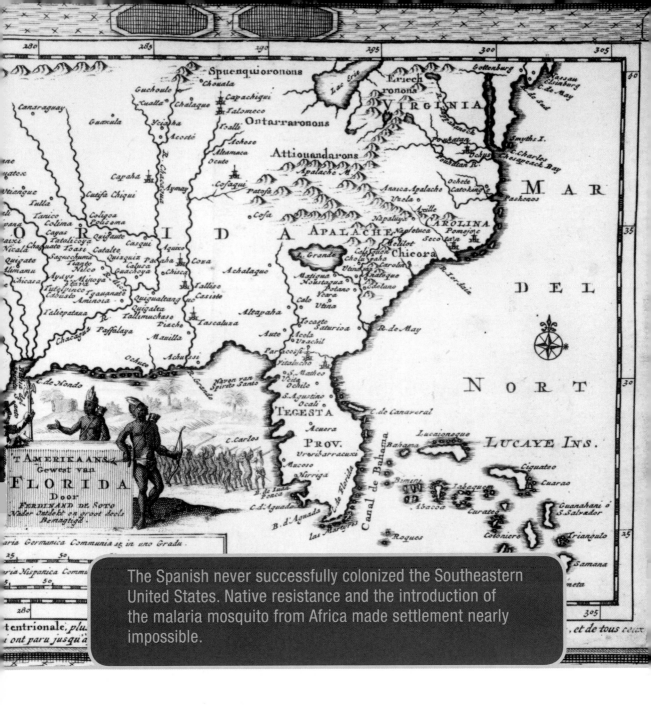

The Spanish never successfully colonized the Southeastern United States. Native resistance and the introduction of the malaria mosquito from Africa made settlement nearly impossible.

Spanish, but Añasco claimed they had informed him that they knew where plenty of gold could be found.

THE RESCUE OF JUAN ORTIZ

On May 18, 1539, de Soto's nine ships set sail for Florida carrying 600 soldiers, 240 horses, and a herd of several hundred Spanish pigs, which he intended to use as a traveling food bank. Many of the pigs escaped and bred freely. They are the ancestors of the wild razorback hogs that roam the American South to this day.

The fleet reached the harbor at Tampa Bay on May 25. De Soto went ashore and settled into a deserted Timucua village named Uzita. One day, de Soto pursued a small group of natives until one of them called out in Spanish, "Sirs, do not kill me, I am a Christian! Like you!" Juan Ortiz was a

De Soto arrived in Tampa Bay, near where the Narváez expedition had met fierce resistance from the warriors of the Apalachee tribal confederacy.

young hidalgo from Seville. He had been a sailor on the Narváez expedition but was captured. He learned the Timucua language but soon escaped to the neighboring Mocoso tribe. Ortiz became the translator of the expedition.

GOLDEN GOOSE CHASE

De Soto was disappointed to learn that Juan Ortiz had seen no gold. But the chief of the Mocoso village told of a town called Urriparacoxi where there was much gold. De Soto marched his army north. The chiefs there sent de Soto gifts of corn and told him of yet another town, Ocali, where the Spanish should find gold. De Soto found only another empty Timucua village. By October, the army reached the lands of the Apalachee Nation in northern Florida. It was here that the Narváez expedition had disappeared.

On October 6, de Soto reached the town of Anhaica only to find it empty and made his

Starvation was an immediate danger to the expedition. European armies usually took food from local people as they marched.

winter camp. He ordered Juan de Añasco to carry a message to the main fleet waiting in Uzita. Añasco took thirty horsemen and covered 500 hundred miles (804 kilometers) in eleven days. The fleet was not happy to be ordered to march toward a land where no gold had been found.

WINTER IN ANHAICA

Near Anhaica, Juan Ortiz, the translator, found a captive sixteen-year-old boy, whom he named Perico. Perico could speak Timucua as well as the Muskogee language. Ortiz could then translate into Spanish. Perico told Ortiz that gold could be found in the north in a rich land called Cofitachequi, which was ruled by a great queen. As the army marched through Georgia, it became clear that Perico had no idea where he was leading them. De Soto was angry, but Perico was too valuable to punish.

In the spring of 1540, the army was on the brink of starvation. In May, the Spanish finally reached the town of Cofitachequi, which was built with temples on high earth mounds.

The Mississippian cultures that de Soto encountered in Georgia were much better organized and armed than the peoples he had previously conquered.

Here they were greeted by the queen, who offered the hungry Spanish corn, beans, and pumpkins and gave them freshwater pearls and "yellow metal," which was native copper, cold hammered into beautiful ceremonial objects of the Mound Builder culture.

BATTLE OF MABILA

De Soto made the queen his prisoner as his army crossed the Appalachian Mountains into North Carolina, searching for copper mines in Chalaque, Ocute, and Chisca. The queen led them ever deeper into the Smoky Mountains, until one day she disappeared into the woods, never to be seen again.

In the summer of 1540, de Soto reached the land of Coosa (in modern Alabama) perhaps the strongest Native American kingdom in the south at that time. The town featured three high earth pyramids surrounded by mud and log walls for protection. De Soto and his men spent the summer in Coosa helping themselves to

The early conquistadors were brutal. Enslavement and torture of Native Americans led the Catholic Church to recommend converting Native Americans to Christianity at missions and plantations called *encomiendas*.

whatever food could be found—the Spanish supply strategy was basically "finders, keepers." As usual, de Soto made a prisoner of the chief of Coosa, who then led de Soto to search for gold in the land of his enemy, Tuscaloosa, in the town of Atahachi.

De Soto promptly made Tuscaloosa his prisoner and demanded corn. Tuscaloosa said that the supplies of food were stored in the town of Mabila.

Tuscaloosa planned to use de Soto's own tactics against the Spanish—it was as if Atahualpa's spirit had returned for revenge. He had already sent word out to thousands of warriors to gather in hiding in and around Mabila. When de Soto arrived on October 13, 1540, with a small delegation of Spaniards, the Mabila chief presented the Spanish officers with a great feast. Suddenly Tuscaloosa's warriors burst from their hiding places and overwhelmed de Soto and his guards. Only de Soto's quilted armor kept him safe until more Spanish arrived. The battle lasted nine hours before the Spanish finally burned the town. More than a thousand Mabilans were dead, but

Chief Tuscaloosa used de Soto's own military tricks against the Spanish by luring them into a trap at Mabila.

the Spanish had lost almost all of their supplies in the fire. Twenty-five conquistadors were dead and half the army had arrow wounds.

DE SOTO FLEES TO THE WEST

For weeks, de Soto's badly wounded army waited at Mabila for a fleet of supply ships from Cuba to arrive. Juan Ortiz learned from local natives that the ships were only a six-day march away, but de Soto told Ortiz to tell no one. De Soto feared his men would desert him and sail back to Cuba, thus ending his search for treasure.

The great Spanish army traveled west through Alabama as winter closed in. Their European clothing was almost gone and most were now dressed in furs and deerskin. When they reached the village of Chicasa, they remained for the winter.

In March, Chickasaw warriors launched a surprise night attack on the camp. Flaming arrows burned de Soto's headquarters to the

Native American villages were often protected by log walls, called palisades, for defense. The Chickasaw people were famous for their fierceness.

ground, and with it, most of the remaining Spanish weapons, tools, and 400 pigs. The 450 surviving Spanish battled their way west, pursued by the fierce Chickasaws every step of the way.

ACROSS THE MIGHTY MISSISSIPPI

On May 8, 1541, de Soto became the first European to cross the Mississippi River. He crossed near Memphis, Tennessee. He built rafts to ferry his men across the Mississippi and reached the town of Casqui. The chief welcomed the Spanish and allowed them to place a cross on the temple mound. Today, this site is a National Historic Landmark in Parkin, Arkansas, and one of the few places where archaeologists have found evidence—glass beads—of de Soto's expedition.

By the fall, the Spanish had advanced on the Kansas plains, where they met their military match in a fierce people they called the Tula, the ancestors of modern Caddo

Although not the first European to see the Mississippi River, de Soto was the first to view and cross it upriver from its mouth at the Gulf of Mexico.

and Pawnee peoples. De Soto had no idea that he was only 200 miles (322 km) distant from another Spanish army, led by Francisco Vázquez de Coronado, who was searching for Cibola, the legendary city of gold hinted at by Cabeza de Vaca. The desolate western plains convinced both conquistadors that it was time to turn around and head home.

THE FINAL BATTLE

The exhausted Spanish army spent the winter of 1541–1542 in Arkansas. Juan Ortiz died, leaving the expedition unable to communicate or negotiate with locals. De Soto still believed that gold could be found, but there was not enough food on the dry plains to support his exhausted army. He led them back to the Mississippi River, where he knew they could plunder villages for food. From there, de Soto hoped to return to Cuba, resupply, and return to continue his quest for gold.

By the spring, de Soto's health gave out. He gathered his soldiers, thanked them for enduring hardship with him, begged forgiveness for his sins, and named his old friend from Peru, Luis de Moscoso, as his successor. On May 21, 1542, Hernando de Soto died of fever, as had so many of the Native Americans who had crossed his path. His men wrapped him in a blanket and sank his body in the Mississippi River.

THE SURVIVORS RETURN

The surviving conquistadors tried to cross the plains headed toward Mexico in the summer of 1542, but starvation caused them to return to the Mississippi, where they spent a winter building boats to carry them down the Mississippi. In September 1543, they landed on the Mexican coast at Panuco. Only 311 Spanish survived.

Spain ceded Florida to the United States in 1821. Today, the state remains a vibrant center for Spanish language and Hispanic culture in North America.

The real legacy of de Soto's expedition was the near total destruction caused by European epidemic diseases introduced to Native American civilizations in the

Bold, ambitious, ruthless, and stubborn: Hernando de Soto's historic legacy in North America is overshadowed by his legend.

southeastern United States. The Mound Builders culture of the Mississippians and their trade networks crumbled. In the two hundred years that followed the expedition, native communities reorganized into the peoples we know today: Muskogee Creeks, Yuchis, Choctaws, Chickasaws, Seminoles, Caddos, and Tunicas, among others. These Native American communities all remain true survivors of the de Soto expedition.

GLOSSARY

archaeology The scientific study of the material remains of past human life and activities.

arquebuses Early guns fired from the shoulder like rifles that were invented in Spain around 1450.

caravel A large medieval sailing ship.

Chickasaw A Native American nation originally from Mississippi and Tennessee.

colony A country or area controlled politically by a more powerful country that is often far away.

conquistador Any of the leaders in the Spanish conquest of America, especially of Mexico and Peru, in the sixteenth century.

epidemic The appearance of a disease in a large number of people at the same time.

hidalgo A hereditary Spanish noble.

immunity The process by which resistance to disease is acquired or caused in plants and animals.

Mississippians A highly developed culture that flourished between 1000 and 1550 CE in the southeastern United States.

plunder Stolen goods.

sling A weapon consisting of a small strap or socket of leather to which two cords were attached, which propels a flying stone with great force.

Timucua An extinct Native American people who once inhabited most of central and northern Florida.

veteran A soldier who has served in a war.

Hernando de Soto Historical Society
910 Third Avenue West
Bradenton, FL 34205
(941) 747-1998
Website: http://www.desotohq.com
The Hernando De Soto Society celebrates the historical
significance of de Soto and sponsors cultural events
such as the annual De Soto Heritage Festival.

Hispanic Society of America
613 West 155th Street
New York, NY 10032
(212) 926-2234
Website: http://www.hispanicsociety.org
The Hispanic Society of America maintains a museum
and reference library for the study of the history, arts,
and cultures of Spain and Latin America.

Muscogee (Creek) Nation Cultural Center
106 West 6th Street
Okmulgee, OK 74447
(918) 549-2434.
Website: http://creekculturalcenter.com
The Creek Cultural Center tells the stories of the original
Native American inhabitants of Georgia and Alabama
after their forced removal to Oklahoma in 1836.

Parkin Archeological State Park
PO Box 1110
Parkin, AR 72373
(870) 755-2500
Website: http://www.arkansasstateparks.com/
    parkinarcheological
The Parkin site may have been the American Indian village
    of Casqui visited by de Soto's expedition in 1541.

United States Park Service De Soto National Memorial
PO Box 15390
Bradenton, FL 34280
(941) 792-0458
Website: https://www.nps.gov/deso/index.htm
Located on the site of Uzita, the De Soto National Memorial
    tells the story of the expedition. Visitors can attend living
    history demonstrations, try on armor, or walk a nature
    trail through a Florida coastal landscape.

Websites

Because of the changing nature of internet links, Rosen
Publishing has developed an online list of websites
related to the subject of this book. This site is updated
regularly. Please use this link to access the list:

http://www.rosenlinks.com/SEC/soto

Clark, Larry Richard. *La Florida: Imperial Spain Invades Indian Chiefdoms of North America 1513–1543.* Morganton, NC: Time Span Press, 2015.

Diamond, Jared M. *Guns, Germs, and Steel: The Fate of Human Societies.* New York, NY: Norton and Company, 2005.

Horwitz, Tony. *A Voyage Long and Strange: Rediscovering the New World.* New York, NY: Henry Holt and Company, 2008.

Hudson, Charles M. *Conversations with the High Priest of Coosa.* Chapel Hill, NC: University of North Carolina Press, 2005.

Mann, Charles C. *1491: New Revelations of the Americas before Columbus.* New York, NY: Vintage Books, 2006.

Mann, Charles C. *1493: Uncovering the New World Columbus Created.* New York, NY. Alfred Knopf, 2011.

Putnam, John Rose. *The River of Corn: Conquistadors Clash with Native Americans.* Kindle Edition, 2014.

White, Ashley. *1539: Artifacts and Archaeology from Conquistador Hernando De Soto's Potano Encampment and the Lost Franciscan Mission.* London, UK: Academic Press Journal, 2015.

BIBLIOGRAPHY

Clayton, Lawrence (editor). *The De Soto Chronicles: The Expedition of Hernando de Soto to North America in 1539–1543.* Tuscaloosa, AL: University of Alabama Press, 1993.

Duncan, David Ewing. *Hernando de Soto: A Savage Quest in the Americas.* New York, NY: Crown Publishers, 1995.

Ethbridge, Robbie, ed. *Mapping the Mississippian Shatter Zone: The Colonial Indian Slave Trade and Regional Instability in the American South.* Lincoln, NE: University of Nebraska Press, 2009.

Ethbridge, Robbie, and Charles Hudson, eds. *The Transformation of the Southeastern Indians 1540–1750.* Oxford, MS: University Press of Mississippi, 2002.

Galloway, Patricia. *The Hernando de Soto Expedition: History, Historiography, and "Discovery" in the Southeast.* Lincoln, NE: University of Nebraska Press 1997.

Hudson, Charles M. *Knights of Spain, Kingdom of the Sun.* Athens, GA: University of Georgia Press, 1997.

Stannard, David. *American Holocaust: The Conquest of the New World.* New York, NY: Oxford University Press, 1992.

Swanton, John R. *The Indians of the Southeastern United States.* Washington, DC: Smithsonian Institution Press, 1946.

INDEX

About the Author

Robert Z. Cohen was born in New York City and studied cultural anthropology and African Studies at Boston University in Boston, Massachusetts. He worked around the Caribbean researching linguistic memories of African languages and spent several years studying Quechua, the language of the Inca people. Cohen moved to Budapest, Hungary, to research the language and music of the Romani (Gypsy) people. He works as an editor, journalist, and travel guide writer and leads his own klezmer band on tours around Europe and North America.

Photo Credits